# SHARKS

## SAVAGE PREDATORS OF THE OCEANS

# SHARKS
## SAVAGE PREDATORS OF THE OCEANS

John McIntyre

𝑝

This is a Parragon Publishing Book

First published in 2006

Parragon Publishing
Queen Street House
4 Queen Street
Bath BA1 1HE, UK

Copyright © Parragon Books Ltd 2006

Designed, produced, and packaged by Stonecastle Graphics Ltd

Text by John McIntyre
Edited by Philip de Ste. Croix
Designed by Sue Pressley and Paul Turner

ISBN 1-40546-374-0

Printed in China

# CONTENTS

# INTRODUCTION

The mere mention of the word 'shark' conjures up a myriad of primeval emotions. It is one of the few animals that can strike fear into our hearts yet simultaneously leave us in awe. Sharks are creatures of myth and legend; stunning predators whose classic, streamlined bodies have evolved over more than 400 million years. Many species have almost reached the point of physical perfection for survival in the world's oceans.

Ask anyone for their views about the majority of animals on our planet and the response may well be ambivalent. But if you ask someone what they think about sharks, whether in a bar, restaurant, or especially on a beach, the chances are that the reaction will be instant. Opinions are likely to range from one extreme to another. The least informed, but sadly often voiced, comment is that 'the best kind of shark is a dead shark.'

My name is John McIntyre and I am a BBC journalist and veteran diver who has spent many hundreds of hours underwater often in close proximity to sharks. My enthusiasm for and fascination with sharks began as a teenager when my parents took me to see the ground-breaking film *Blue Water, White Death*. During a varied career, I have reported for the BBC on the controversy of cage diving with great whites, broadcast live from inside one of Europe's biggest shark tanks, and produced the film *Sharks: The Big Ten* featuring some of the best shark action in the world's oceans. In writing this book, I want to give a non-sensationalist appraisal of the many types of sharks roaming our seas and explain why it is important to understand the reasons behind some of the terrifying incidents involving this most dangerous but impressive of apex predators.

I believe sharks are among the most beautiful and awesome of all the animals on Earth. Being in the water with sharks is about as close as it's possible to get to nature in its ultimate form. This is why it is so vital that we do everything we can to afford the shark the protection it deserves.

Already a greater understanding of sharks is leading to an increasingly positive attitude to them; people now recognize that they are in fact creatures of great stealth and dynamism without which the marine environment would suffer enormously. People do of course get bitten, even killed, and the headlines scream out reports of such incidents. But these tragic events are fortunately remarkably few in number.

A good friend of mine who spent years photographing sharks all over the world borrows a well-known line from Shakespeare to make the point that in recent evolutionary history man is now the shark's main enemy – 'sharks are far more sinned against than sinning.'

There are thought to be about 450 different types of shark roaming the world's seas. They vary greatly in size, appearance, and biology. There are sharks that lay eggs, others that give birth to live, fully formed replicas of their parents. There are even sharks which become cannibals inside the womb, eating their siblings as a means of survival.

The world's biggest and second biggest fish are both sharks, yet neither is a meat eater. They are respectively the giant whale shark and the basking shark. They grow to the size of a school bus yet live on the tiniest creatures in the sea, plankton. Amazingly, it's only now thanks to satellite tracking and computer technology that we are starting to gain an understanding about how these huge creatures live.

There are no prizes for guessing the shark which gets all the headlines and the notoriety. Yes, there is only one Number One – the great white shark. It is also known as white pointer and white death. If there is one predator on Earth which commands our ultimate respect, it must surely be the great white, one of the most ruthless killers in the sea. It is not difficult to understand why man is so fearful of this 20-foot beast. Could it be that we feel an instinctive terror at the thought of an animal with big, sharp teeth capable of biting us in two without effort?

The one word which has come to symbolize this fear and continues to haunt the shark to this day is *Jaws.*' This innovative adventure movie thrilled audiences but demonized sharks to the point where it provoked considerable numbers of 'revenge' killings by people who felt threatened by their mere existence.

Amazingly, many people who have suffered terrible wounds inflicted by sharks take a different view – they defend their potential killers, recognizing that they are amazing animals which deserve our respect and protection.

In parts of the world – notably Australia and South Africa – laws have been introduced to protect the great white shark. In the UK, legislation has been enacted to help save the giant, but harmless, basking shark.

Whatever your personal view, I hope you will agree that the story of the shark is truly incredible.

**Left:** Author John McIntyre filming underwater.
**Above:** John gets up close and personal with a Caribbean reef shark (*Carcharhinus perezi*) in the warm waters of the Bahamas.

# SHARK EVOLUTION

If someone asked you to describe the perfect killing machine, the chances are that the first thing you would think of would be the shark. Nothing is left to chance in the friendless world of this superlative apex predator. Nor does the shark possess even the smallest biological characteristic which is unnecessary. Every inch of the shark's body, its external shape and internal organs, have evolved for one purpose – to catch food in order to survive. Over some four hundred million years, evolution has honed every last detail. Today some 450 different kinds of shark populate the oceans, and they vary greatly in shape and size.

A good example is the strange anvil-shaped head of the scalloped hammerhead shark. Some scientists believe this creature may be the most developed of all the sharks. Its wide flattened head, with eyes at either end, acts rather like both a metal detector and a hydrofoil, providing the shark with maximum sensory input while at the same time providing superb maneuverability.

Such weird and wonderful features in sharks have been evolving since before the time of the dinosaurs. Some sharks, however, have inevitably gone the way of the dinosaurs and are now extinct. The most famous of these is *Carcharodon megalodon*, a true giant with jaws so large that, if it were alive today, it would be able to swallow a man who was standing up. Each tooth was as big as a human hand. Fossilized megaladon teeth are now prized collector's items.

In piecing together the jigsaw of the shark story, scientists have gleaned much of their information from the fossilized remains of these ancient fish, and especially from their teeth which are often perfectly preserved. Often only the fossilized teeth remain to be found because sharks belong to a family of animals which do not have a bony skeleton. Instead their frames are made of a tough, flexible material called cartilage. They have, therefore, been assigned to the scientific group named *elasmobranchs* which includes the rays and some of the lesser-known fish which live in the constant darkness of the ocean abyss. Having a cartilaginous frame is akin to a sports car designer using strong but lightweight carbon fiber for the vehicle's chassis. In the case of the

shark, the design is really the product of the revolutionary forces of nature. Another crucial difference between sharks and bony fish is that sharks do not have swim bladders. A swim bladder in a fish acts rather like a diver's buoyancy control jacket. As the diver goes deeper and the water pressure increases, he or she simply pumps more air into the jacket to maintain neutral buoyancy and so remain at the chosen depth.

The shark, however, relies on having a very large liver containing fine oil which is lighter than water and which aids buoyancy. Even with this large liver, the shark is still heavier than water and will naturally sink. This is why sharks have to swim constantly every day of their lives. There are a few exceptions to this rule but in general sharks have to keep on the move to survive. Like birds riding the wind, sharks are masters of the ocean currents. They glide through the water with minimum effort, saving their hard-earned fuel for those crucial bursts of speed when hunting prey.

Despite the small size of its brain, the shark's evolutionary credentials as the number one marine killer read like the specification for a deadly military machine from the future.

Perhaps the most extraordinary of all the shark's weaponry are the acute sensory organs which appear like tiny dots on the snout. These are actually tiny cavities filled with a jelly-like substance which are capable of detecting the smallest of electrical currents. These electro-receptors are known as 'ampullae of Lorenzini.' When a fish is struggling or dying, its muscles emit barely perceptible electrical signals. Even at distance, the shark picks these up. Witnessing this behavior in the Bahamas, I was amazed at both the distances involved and the frenzied

**Previous pages**

Page 8: The savage-looking dental apparatus of the sand tiger shark (*Carcharias taurus*) whose fearsome appearance belies its normally docile character.

Page 9: A great hammerhead (*Sphyrna mokarran*) patrolling the Bahamas near the surface providing an excellent view of its hydrofoil-shaped head.

A five-million-year-old fossilized tooth from the world's biggest ever shark *Carcharodon megalodon*.

speed with which Caribbean reef sharks react to small fish lying injured on a reef.

So it is understandable that the quest to develop a reliable system of anti-shark protection finally achieved success when electricity was harnessed as a means of defense. By generating relatively strong electrical fields around a diver, scientists have found that they can effectively jam the shark's senses and cause even the biggest of sharks to turn away.

There is also a fine line which runs along the entire length of the shark's body. It is known as the lateral line. This enables a shark to detect minute vibrations in the water around it and so sense the presence of other animals in the water. Even the smallest of magnetic fields in the sea can be detected by the shark's sophisticated array of senses, helping them to navigate with accuracy.

Sharks have excellent eyesight, superb sensitivity to sound, and, of course, a perfect sense of smell. As an amazing example of their olfactory abilities, it is known that sharks can detect a single drop of blood in one million drops of water.

Perfection characterizes everything about shark evolution. The skin is another ingenious design. It is covered in thousands of rows of tiny modified teeth called dermal denticles. If you rub your hand from snout to tail, a shark's skin feels silky smooth. Rub it in the opposite direction and you could easily tear your own skin to pieces. This amazing design feature not only gives the shark a tough outer protection, it also gives the animal excellent streamlining in water. Like all the best designs in nature, man has copied it. The shark-skin suit has been tried and tested to great effect by swimmers, allowing them to slip through the water with considerably reduced drag.

Since sharks are the apex predator in all areas of the world's oceans, they have had to adapt to their local environments. There are sharks for every occasion. The angel shark, for example, lurks in the sand at the bottom of the ocean like a silent trap waiting to gulp unsuspecting prey that swim nearby. Saw sharks have bizarre serrated snouts which often look like medieval weapons. There are goblin sharks, crocodile sharks, catsharks, thresher sharks, and so the list goes on. The design of each has been modified by evolution over millions of years to ensure survival in the most extreme of circumstances, whether in the abyssal plains of the deep, the rocky shallows, coral reefs, or out in mid-ocean. Sharks roam every corner of the globe from the near-freezing waters of the Arctic to the warm Caribbean reefs.

Some sharks give birth to live young, while others lay eggs. And not all sharks are dangerous to man – the biggest of the world's sharks are actually totally harmless. Both the giant whale shark and its close cousin, the basking shark, live on the smallest of prey, plankton and small fish.

Sharks are indeed masterpieces of evolution. If a computer today were to be programed to design the perfect underwater killing machine, we should not be surprised if the answer looked remarkably like a shark.

The sand tiger shark (*Carcharias taurus*) was the first species to receive legal protection in Australia in 1984.

**Above:** The horn shark (*Heterodontus francisci*) grows to only 3 feet (1m) in length and is ideally adapted for hunting in rocky areas of the Pacific. This shows just how well shark species have evolved to suit their particular environments.

**Right:** The shortfin mako (*Isurus oxyrinchus*) is one of the fastest swimming sharks in the ocean, capable of hunting down agile tuna and marlin. This specimen was photographed in the Red Sea.

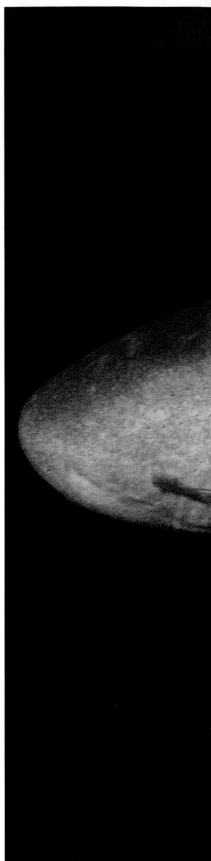

**Above:** Whitetip reef sharks (*Triaenodon obesus*) are common in the world's tropical oceans. They are almost entirely benign around humans but tireless pack hunters of prey fish at night.

**Right:** Blue sharks (*Prionace glauca*) can grow to around 12 feet (3.7m) in length and live in the mid-ocean. They are one of the most elegant of sharks and a favorite among photographers.

**Opposite:** Sand tiger sharks (*Carcharias taurus*) are favorite aquarium fish because they are relatively easy to keep and those teeth cannot fail to impress.

Scalloped hammerheads (*Sphyrna lewini*) often school in vast numbers around natural sea mounds in places like Cocos, off the coast of Costa Rica. In these areas they queue up to be cleaned of parasites by butterfly fish.

Great hammerheads (*Sphyrna mokarran*) are among the rarest of sharks to be seen or photographed. They can grow to around 20 feet (6m) in length and can weigh up to about 1000lb (450kg). They are known to eat other smaller sharks and rays as part of their diet.

This stunning picture of a great hammerhead was taken head-on in the Bahamas by underwater photographer Charles Hood. It looks almost like a high-tech fighter aircraft with its all-searching eyes approximately five feet (1.5m) apart. Great hammerheads are particularly fond of eating stingrays. They use their broad heads to pin a ray down on the seabed and then immobilize it by biting a piece out of its pectoral wing.

# CLASSIC SHARKS

The classic, sleek lines of certain sharks have made them the 'supermodels' of the sea. Just as a stunning human model can boost the circulation of a magazine, diving and natural history publications have found that sales increase dramatically when a shark is chosen as the cover shot. One of the most photographed is the reef shark and it is without doubt the most easily identifiable. They range from the feisty Caribbean reef shark to the ubiquitous gray reef shark. These two species and some of their similar looking relatives are largely found in tropical seas. There are, of course, many subtle physical variations depending on the area of world in which they are encountered.

As a basic guide, the classic shape of a shark is a long, grayish or brownish torpedo-like body with a white underbelly. The usual configuration features five gill slits and eight fins, the most recognizable of which is the first dorsal − this is the one which often protrudes from the water and 'scares the living daylights' out of startled bathers. The fins next to the gill slits are known as pectorals, while the tailfin goes under the scientific name of caudal. Four more, smaller fins complete the set. Male sharks possess two claspers which are extensions of the pelvic fins − these are the sex organs but, in case you were wondering, they only use one at a time.

The classic species belong to a family known as the requiem sharks (*Carcharhinidae*) which accounts for more than half of the known shark populations. As a result of their wide distribution, these sharks statistically account for the majority of human deaths and injuries caused by shark attacks. The most famous 'classic' shark of all, the great white, doesn't actually belong to this family group but is a mackerel shark (*Lamnidae*), so this ultimate predator has been given a chapter of its own − see page 76.

The family of requiem sharks includes species that will be familiar to any viewer of natural history documentaries − the powerful bull shark, the beautifully elongated blue shark, and the heavyweight 'trashcan of the ocean,' the tiger shark.

As the majority stakeholders in the ocean's apex community, requiem sharks play a vital role in keeping their environment well balanced. It is

their function to hunt down and eat sick, injured, and weak prey. This is nothing more than a demonstration of the ruthless nature of the survival of the fittest in action.

Some of these sharks, especially the smaller whitetip reef sharks, hunt in packs like wild dogs. At night they scour the reefs seeking out the slightest movement of their quarry. One of the best places in the world to observe this behavior is the remote Pacific island of Cocos. Here whitetips congregate in their hundreds, patrolling the rocky undersea terrain like gangs of delinquent teenagers strutting their stuff on the streets. When a fish is targeted, the sharks bombard the reef. Their skin is so tough that they can squeeze their heads into the smallest of nooks and crannies and emerge unscathed. After a night of frenzied activity, they spend the day either resting on the seafloor or riding the thermoclines around the island. Whitetips are among the few sharks able to pump water over their gills in order to breathe while remaining still.

Whitetips and the more classically shaped gray reef shark are frequently seen by divers. While the whitetip is extremely docile, the grays can be aggressive when provoked. They grow to just over 6 feet (2m). They spend the days on the move and likewise hunt at night. But woe betide the diver who dares to push his or her luck too far. When a gray shark feels threatened in any way, it adopts a highly-charged posture. First the shark lowers its pectoral fins. If the diver − or other shark for that matter − does not get the message, then the animal goes to the next level. This involves arching its back. When a shark displays these two threat postures, it is time to back off or suffer the consequences. The shark can strike with lightning speed and the consequent injuries can be very nasty.

**Previous pages**

Page 22: Reef shark in classic pose with a remora on its underbelly.

Page 23: The blacktip reef shark (*Carcharhinus melanopterus*) is a common inhabitant of lagoons and reefs in the Pacific and Indian oceans. These are seen in the waters off Tahiti.

Progressing up the requiem hierarchy, we encounter one of the most dangerous sharks in the world − the muscle-bound bull shark. At up to 11 feet (3.5m) in length, the bull shark looks as though it is on steroids. Bulls are far more likely to kill people than almost all other sharks including the great white. One reason for this is that they have the rare ability to move between seawater and fresh water. Bull sharks have been discovered many miles inland in murky rivers. Where local inhabitants are forced to make a living from the river − in places like South Africa and South America − the risk of shark attack is considerable. Many incidents go unreported due to the remote location of these villages.

At the top of the requiem pyramid is the awesome tiger shark. These sharks have been known to devour pretty well anything and everything that they encounter in their hunt for food. Dead specimens have been found to have a bizarre range of stomach contents − car license plates, a boy's shinbone, antlers, dogs, tin cans, and even car tires have been found.

Some of the largest recorded tiger sharks have been measured at over 18 feet (5-6m). As their name suggests, they are easily identified by their tiger-like markings. Initially these predators may appear cautious and shy, but make no mistake: this is not a shark to misjudge.

While tigers tend to be seen in twos and threes − though often they are solitary − other members of the requiem family gather in force. Again in the food-rich waters around Cocos, the extremely photogenic silky shark is sometimes seen in vast schools. This type of shark is referred to as 'oceanic' or 'pelagic,' meaning that they spend most of their lives in the open ocean.

When it comes to reproduction, requiem sharks share a trait with mammals. Not only do they fertilize their eggs internally, they also give birth to live, fully formed miniature sharks. In order to reproduce, the male shark bites the female with its blade-like teeth and locks on while mating. Females often bear the scars that result, which are sometimes referred to as 'love bites.'

A gray reef shark may give birth to between one and six pups after a long gestation period that lasts about a year.

If there is a weakness in the shark's domination of the world's oceans, this is it. It can take up to seven years for a shark to reach sexual maturity. In areas where shark stocks are heavily depleted through over-fishing (especially for the purposes of making shark-fin soup) it is difficult, and in some cases impossible, for those populations to be sustained. Accurate scientific data about shark numbers are difficult to obtain but there are many conservation organizations – as well as the United Nations Environment Program – which are convinced that unless there is a massive reduction in this industry, the days of the classic shark may be numbered.

The silky shark (*Charcarhinus falciformis*) is a large, slender, oceanic shark that grows up to 10 feet (3.3m) in length. They are often seen swimming in vast schools in deep water where they hunt for squid and fish.

**Left:** Gray reef sharks (*Carcharhinus amblyrhynchos*) can be bad tempered when provoked. They are often seen in strong currents in places like the Red Sea, the Maldives, and Australia.

**Above:** This stunning oceanic whitetip shark (*Carcharhinus longimanus*) was photographed in the Egyptian Red Sea and is accompanied by ever-present pilot fish which are thought to feed on scraps that are left over from the shark's meal. In areas where they share the same habitat, oceanic whitetips are often found swimming with big pods of pilot whales, and will even follow the whales when they dive into deep water.

Blacktip reef sharks
(*Carcharhinus melanopterus*)
are often found using schools
of barracuda as cover, as
shown here at Ras Mohamed
in the Red Sea where they are
regularly sighted in the
summer months.

The tiger shark (*Galeocerdo cuvier*) grows up to 18 feet (5.5m) in length and has a reputation for being the garbage bin of the world's oceans, eating virtually anything it can swallow in its hunt for food. Tiger sharks are regarded as being potentially dangerous to both bathers and divers.

These small fish are hitching a ride on the pressure wave created by a gray reef shark in the Bahamas. This is an excellent way to get a free ride and to pick up scraps of food that are left over when the host has fed.

Caribbean reef sharks
(*Carcharhinus perezi*) are
probably the most
photographed of all sharks
since they seem largely
unconcerned by the presence
of divers. They are gray to
grayish-brown in color with
white undersides and grow to
a length of about 10 feet (3m).

Shark feeds are big business. It is calculated that each live shark is worth about US$100,000 annually to a local economy in terms of the tourism generated by attracting people who want to swim with sharks. In the Maldives, for example, divers spend US$2.3 million a year on shark dives. This is estimated to be worth 100 times more than the export value of the shark meat. These feeding sharks were photographed at Walker's Cay in the Bahamas.

Bull sharks (*Charcharhinus leucas*) are probably the most dangerous sharks in the sea, accounting for more human deaths than any other shark. They are powerful beasts but at Walker's Cay, Bahamas, people snorkel with them in 6 feet (2m) of water. These swimmers are safe because the water is clear and the sharks are interested only in the fish. Their senses are so acute that they can easily distinguish between people and their preferred food. However, in murky water bull sharks are to be avoided at all costs.

Caribbean reef sharks will often approach to within inches of a camera or a diver's mask before turning away at the last second. These sharks are usually considered to be non-aggressive to divers, but instances of attacks on people have been recorded.

# THE BIGGEST SHARKS

Not all sharks are dangerous. In fact the two largest sharks – and therefore the two biggest fish roaming our seas – devour nothing more spectacular than tiny plankton. Both sharks are characterized as gentle giants of the ocean. The larger of the two is the graceful, more photogenic whale shark, so named because of its immense size. The second biggest fish in the sea is the less elegant and slightly more prehistoric-looking basking shark, which is found in colder waters. The biggest programs of current research into these fish are focused on the schools of basking sharks patrolling the shores of Britain.

In the case of the distinctively patterned whale shark, a true sense of its scale is given by the dramatic images of divers or snorkellers trying their best to keep pace with one of these gargantuan creatures. Next time you see a yellow school bus, just imagine a fish swimming alongside it which is the same length. They are known to grow to about 40 feet (12m) in length though there have been reports of monster whale sharks growing to about 60 feet (18m). This would actually make them larger than some of the great whales which are, of course, mammals. While it is difficult to gauge the average weight of the world's biggest fish, specimens have been measured at over 18,000lb (8165kg), with massive livers which alone have tipped the scales at a mighty one ton.

For an animal so large, however, their eyes are relatively small. Like the basking shark, it seems that the greatest virtue of these enormous sharks lies in their huge mouths. They are very similar to whales in this respect. When cruising near the surface in search of their humble diet of plankton and other small creatures, their highly efficient filter-feeding system sifts food from thousands of gallons of water every hour. An underwater filmmaker who was confronted by his first basking shark off the coast of Cornwall could hardly believe his eyes. 'I saw this giant mouth coming toward me. I honestly thought I was going to be swallowed whole.' Fortunately, there was little danger. Neither the whale shark nor the basking shark is capable of consuming anything bigger than the sort of fish that might be served in a restaurant.

Both of these sharks will travel thousands of miles every year in pursuit of their staple diet. Modern-day satellite tagging is increasingly being used to track their movements for scientific research. Oddly enough the whale shark is one of the most difficult animals to find, despite its huge size. In the Red Sea, where the whale shark was captured on film for the first time in 1949 by the pioneering husband and wife diving team of Hans and Lotte Hass, sightings are rare these days. People who have worked as dive guides for ten years or more often report seeing only one or two during their entire career. But there are favored locations for finding this dinosaur of the deep. In a tiny corner of the world known as Ningaloo Reef in northwestern Australia, a small industry has grown around the virtually guaranteed sightings of *Rhincodon typus*, to give its scientific name. For the small band of scientists, tourists, and divers who converge on Ningaloo every February and March, this has become a magical place. This also happens to be the reef where the author first encountered the whale shark.

A combination of climate and favorable currents seem to create the perfect conditions to satisfy the whale shark's relentless appetite. For this is also the time when coral reefs are spawning, turning the surrounding seas into a veritable smorgasbord of micro-organisms to feast upon. Even so, divers still need help in finding the biggest fish in the sea. To ensure a high rate of success, whale shark tour operators make use of light aircraft or microlights to hunt for tell-tale giant shadows meandering through the waters below. The pilot contacts the boat by radio to give an exact position of the shark and tourists are then plunged into the water in the path of the whale shark – sometimes in quite

**Previous pages**

Page 42: A whale shark (*Rhincodon typus*) attracts many fellow travelers including large remoras and schools of fusiliers.

Page 43: A snorkeller is dwarfed by the world's biggest shark but, fear not, it is entirely harmless!

close proximity to the deadlier tiger sharks which have also come to Ningaloo to take advantage of an abundant food chain. Then, for a brief but exhilarating few minutes, the swimmer paddles energetically alongside the mighty whale shark, dwarfed by its presence. It is quite simply an awesome experience. Snorkellers have, however, almost come to grief on occasion, thanks to the practice of riding the shark's fins for thrills. When whale sharks are spooked by over-eager divers, they often plumb the depths. For certain individuals, this leads to a hair-raising experience when they suddenly realize that they are heading into dangerously deep water, desperate to catch a breath. Many operators are now critical of divers who ride sharks, fearing it may have an adverse effect on the animal's behavior. These days in western Australia, a person can be prosecuted for riding a whale shark.

In British waters, the law also protects the whale shark's slightly smaller cousin, the basking shark. In the summer months off the coasts of Cornwall, the Isle of Man, and western Scotland, these lumbering marine grazers make their annual appearance, much to the delight of holidaymakers and scientists. There was a time when their huge fins made them a target for the lucrative shark fin soup market. They were also hunted mercilessly for their large livers, which contain fine oil used for lighting products among other things. Basking shark populations declined significantly, but fortunately those days are now gone, at least in the UK.

However, in the comparatively cold, green seas of the British Isles it has taken many years for people to grow accustomed to the sight of a 6.5 foot (2m) tall charcoal-gray shark fin breaching the surface not so very far from the shoreline. In fact, worried lifeguards peering out to sea have been known to sound the alarm to call people out of the water, fearing a *Jaws* scenario on their watch. Like the whale shark, the basking shark is only interested in the small plankton and crustacean larvae that discolor the seas during the summer months. They too have become tourist attractions, with boat charters seeking out schools of up to 30 or 40 animals that may be slowly but purposefully trawling the English and Irish channels for sustenance. A healthy sized basking shark grows to around 33 feet (10m) in length and has a life span of up to 50 years. Even when born – these sharks give birth to live pups – they already measure an enormous 3 feet (1m) plus, and are ready to take on the world. While a fully grown specimen could cause humans serious harm, they have been known to brush gently past adults and children alike without delivering so much as a glancing blow.

A remarkable research program carried out by British scientists has proved invaluable in solving some of the mysteries of the basking shark. Satellite tagging and photographic studies have shown that the basking sharks seen year after year in UK waters are actually British residents. They may travel large distances around the coast and dive into deeper waters in the winter months, but they remain territorial. This crucial information is helping to protect sharks. Knowing they are resident means the laws protecting them are far more effective than if the animals were simply migratory visitors.

It may not be as glamorous as the biggest fish in the ocean, but the basking shark has also won its fair share of fans. So next time you are on vacation in the British Isles, count yourself lucky if you spot a large dorsal fin close to shore. Far from being a terrifying man-eater, it is actually a harmless local resident that just happens to be a very big shark.

Whale sharks can grow to a giant 60 feet (18m) in length. They travel thousands of miles every year in search of plankton and small fish and squid which they consume in vast quantities.

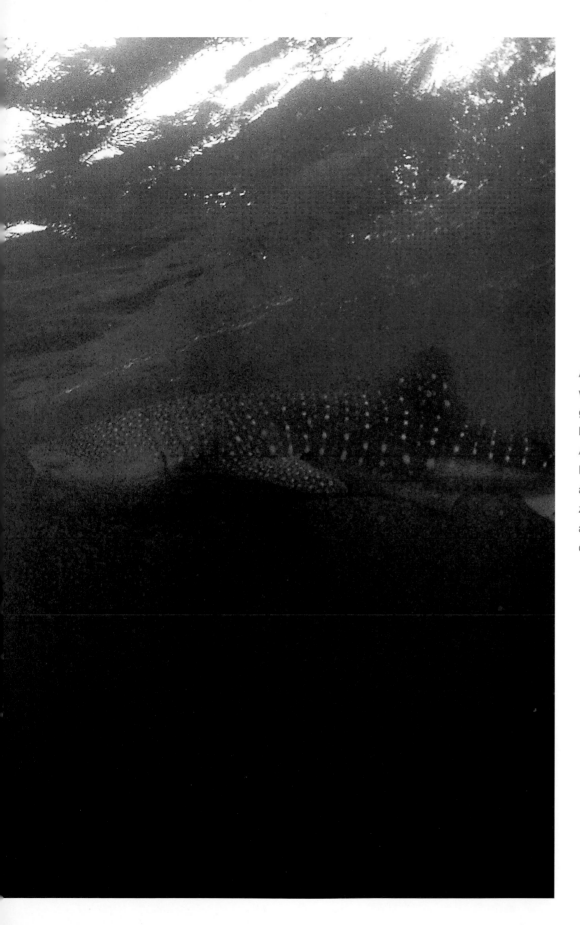

At certain times of the year whale sharks are known to gather off the coast of places like Ningaloo in western Australia, the Seychelles, and Honduras to feast on the abundant blooms of zooplankton and to take advantage of the annual coral spawning.

Despite being the biggest fish
in the ocean, whale sharks are
nevertheless rarely seen. Only
in recent years have satellite
tagging programs started to
yield clues to their behavior
patterns.

**Above:** A whale shark swims in nutrient-rich waters surrounded by a dense school of fusiliers. The presence of these fish indicates a plentiful food supply.

**Right:** Whale sharks are officially protected by a number of countries including Australia, Honduras, India, Philippines, and the USA. However, they are still hunted both legally and illegally in parts of Asia.

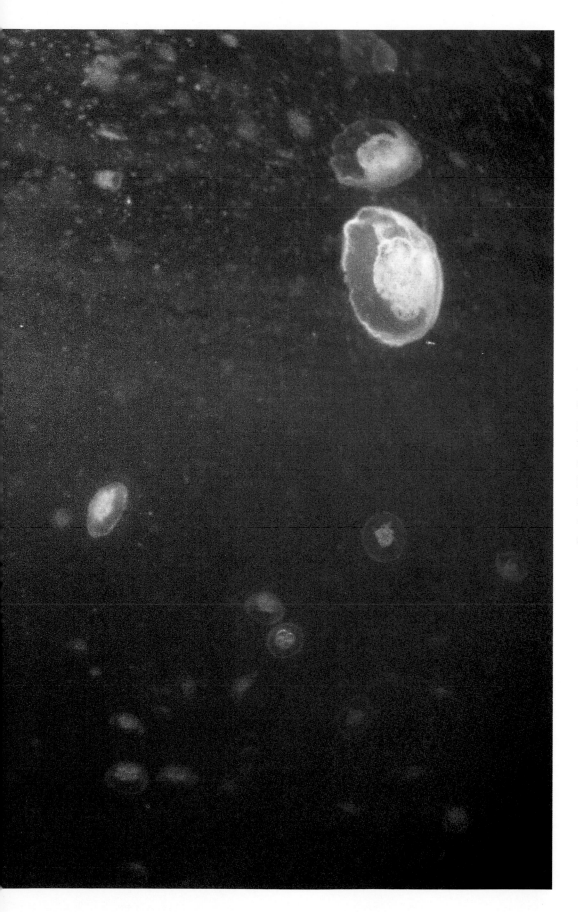

A basking shark (*Cetorhinus maximus*) with its mouth agape filter-feeding on plankton, among jellyfish, off the Isle of Man. These giant sharks sometimes congregate in their hundreds in the summer months and can easily be spotted from the shore in calm seas.

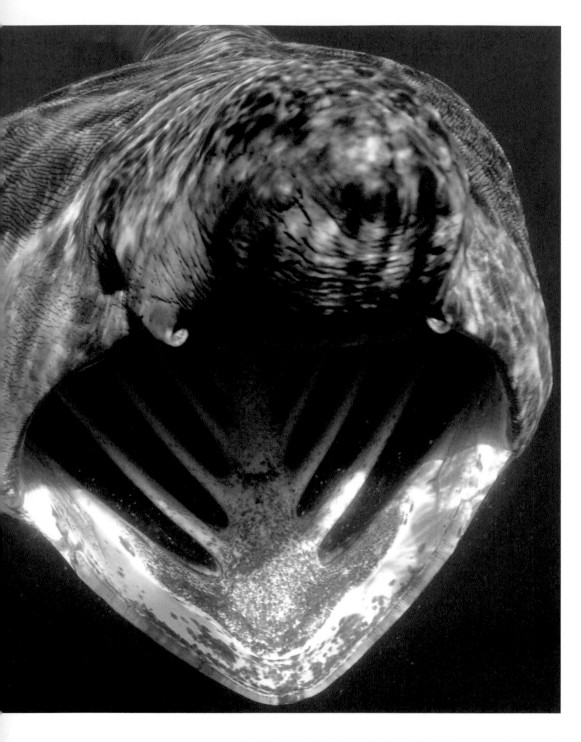

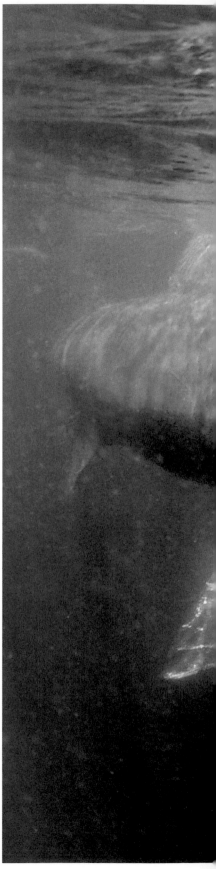

Basking sharks feed by swimming with their huge mouths opened wide, filtering plankton and microscopic animals out of the water using their gill rakers (small bristle-like filtering devices on the gills themselves). The basking shark's gill rakers can strain up to 2000 tons of water per hour. Every so often, a feeding shark will close its gills and 'backflush' the food into its throat, where it is swallowed.

# SHARKS AND PEOPLE

Coming face to face with a shark is listed as one of the top thrills that people would love to experience before they die. Remarkably, four of the top five such activities involve the wonders of our blue planet. While swimming with dolphins is the number one dream, diving with sharks ranks a courageous fifth.

For people who have an innate fear of sharks, the challenge may be extremely difficult – even terrifying – but nowadays arranging it really can be as easy as booking a trip over the internet.

Attitudes to sharks have changed considerably in the past few decades. It is not so long ago that many people believed the 'best shark was a dead shark.' Pioneers of underwater filmmaking were among the very few people 'brave enough' to get into the water with sharks, as so little was known about these potential killers. Decades have passed since the likes of Jacques Cousteau, Hans and Lotte Hass, Stan Waterman, and the Australian couple Ron and Valerie Taylor brought mesmerizing images of the undersea world into our living rooms. Pictures of people swimming in the water with sharks were enough to set pulses racing among television viewers, let alone the uncertain and apprehensive divers.

One famous film, *Blue Water, White Death* (1971), broke new ground as it was the first major documentary to go in search of great white sharks. Peter Gimbel's epic journey took the team halfway round the world but the pictures of the Taylors and other divers leaving the safety of their cages to enter the water as oceanic whitetip sharks were savaging a dead sperm whale were electrifying. The whale carcass failed to attract the great whites but eventually the team succeeded in tracking down the number one beast and the resulting film was widely praised as the most exciting shark movie of its time.

It is hardly surprising then that Hollywood found the lure of the shark irresistible. In the Bahamas, the makers of James Bond movies enrolled local divers to work with Caribbean reef and tiger sharks to create deadly scenarios for their celluloid hero. The films *Never Say Never Again* and *For Your Eyes Only* turned the island of Nassau into one of the first big shark-diving destinations. It was not long before people came

Don't try this at home – even wearing a steel-mesh suit a diver will find a determined blue shark (*Prionace glauca*) more than a match for his strength when food is involved.

from all over the world to pay good money to get within inches of those notorious jaws.

In order for the dive operators to grow their business, however, the incentive had to work both ways. If they were going to make money, then the sharks needed a reason to put on a show. There was only one way – the divers became 'shark wranglers' armed with bucketfuls of fish. The sharks did not take long to realize that they were in for a treat and responded like nervous pets wanting a piece of the action. With dozens of Caribbean reef sharks arriving for dinner – and distinctly lacking in table manners – the divers carrying the food needed protection. It was the likes of Valerie Taylor who tried and tested the steel-mesh suits that are now commonplace on shark feeds around the world.

**Previous pages**

Page 56: A close encounter with a shark is always a memorable experience for any diver.

Page 57: Shark tourism in action: dozens of Caribbean reef sharks (*Carcharhinus perezi*) turn up for a free feed in the Bahamas and provide paying guests with one of the most thrilling wildlife experiences in the process.

There are shark feeds in many tropical locations. For the price of a modest dinner for two it is possible to see how sharks tuck into a menu of tuna and jackfish. These shows run almost daily in places like the Caribbean and Australia. The diver – often protected by a mesh suit or at the very least steel mesh gloves and arm guards – usually carries the 'chum' to the seafloor in a sealed box. Guest divers are then instructed to form a semi-circle about 15-20 feet (5-6m) away from the feeder. Within minutes the reef sharks make an excited appearance. Inexperienced divers often react by breathing heavily, especially when some of the animals literally swim between their legs! Soon the sharks are taking pieces of fish either from the diver's hand or from the tip of a steel rod. At this point it becomes a free-for-all. The sharks will even bump into divers as they compete for the free bounty of fish. There have been incidents where the sharks have bitten the divers by accident – sometimes causing serious wounds – but considering the thousands of dives that take place every year, statistically it is no more dangerous than, say, riding a bicycle.

The reasons why people want to get in the water with sharks varies. Some enjoy the adrenalin rush, others are trying to overcome a phobia, and others see the shark as a potentially dangerous yet beautiful creature to be admired rather than feared. Many people come away with a different attitude to sharks after they have encountered them. The word most often used by shark tourists once the dive is over is 'respect.'

The shark industry is big business. Like whale watching, it has also helped persuade people that a shark is actually worth more alive than dead. It is reckoned that a single live shark can have a value of $100,000 to a local economy generated by eco-tourism.

While Jacques Cousteau may have introduced many of us to the magic of the silent underwater world, the craze for modern day celebrity has spawned thousands of hours of shark television programs fronted by enthusiastic scientists or famous presenters.

Channels devote entire weeks exclusively to sharks, pushing at the boundaries of science and human interaction. At 'Dangerous Reef' in southern Australia and Dyer Island in South Africa, the controversial craze for cage-diving with great whites has been opened up to ordinary tourists. Thrill-seekers enjoy a short but heart-pounding encounter from within the safety of a sturdily built steel cage. Depending on your viewpoint, a 16-foot (4m) great white baring its large teeth and biting at the bars of the cage can be the high point of the dive.

But even this is eclipsed by the activities of a handful of shark experts. People like Andre Hartman first got hearts racing by stroking great whites on the snout as they pushed their heads out of the water to inspect the boats. Hartman and a few others tested their nerves to the limits, however, when they decided to free-dive with great whites with only their wits to protect them. Since a shark can easily detect the quickening beat of a heart, this is not an experience for the nervous. But for any person brave enough a face-to-face encounter with the most notorious predator on Earth must surely rank as one of the ultimate wildlife experiences.

Not for the faint-hearted or the inexperienced! Free-diver Michael Rutzen touches the nose of a great white shark (*Carcharodon carcharias*), South Africa.

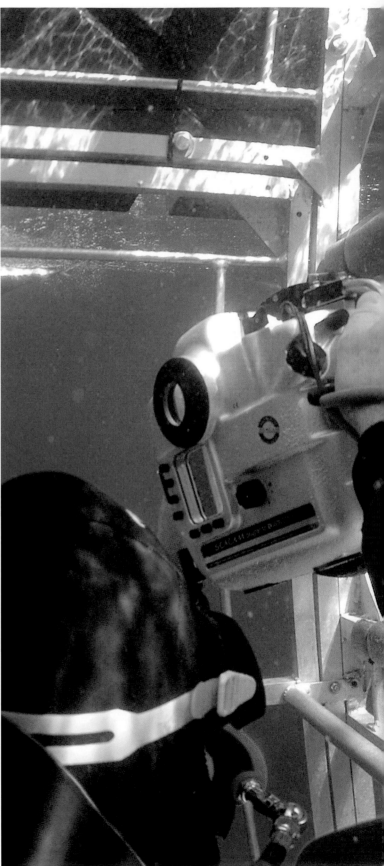

**Above:** Award-winning underwater photographer Douglas David Seifert took these pictures during a great white shark expedition off the coast of the island of Guadalupe, Mexico. This is the big new destination for seeing the number one shark in clear blue water. 'Chum' made from tuna meat, fish blood, and oil is used to attract the sharks close to the cages.

**Right:** A diver views the sharks from the relative safety of a steel cage. This kind of eco-tourism first developed in southern Australia and South Africa where there are large concentrations of great whites.

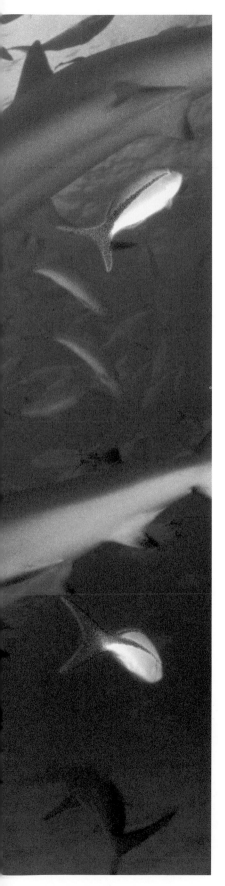

**Left:** Shark feeding in the Bahamas took off as a tourist attraction after Hollywood started making James Bond movies featuring sharks. It soon became apparent that tourists were happy to pay to get in the water with sharks.

**Above:** Next to the perfectly evolved lines of the shark, humans appear out of place. But the privilege of eyeballing a shark is an experience for which people are prepared to pay hundreds of millions of dollars worldwide every year.

Even though this great
hammerhead (*Sphyrna
mokarran*) eats other sharks, it
shows no interest in the diver
approaching to take a picture.
These large sharks are
supremely well adapted for
predation. Each eye can look
at different objects
simultaneously while their
strangely shaped heads act
like metal detectors, picking
up tiny electrical impulses
from the surrounding water.

Some people get to work closely with sharks as a result of scientific studies. Plucky volunteer Mike Braun pushes a tiger shark (*Galeocerdo cuvier*) through the water to revive it after it has been measured and tagged as part of a University of Miami research program in the waters off the Bahamas.

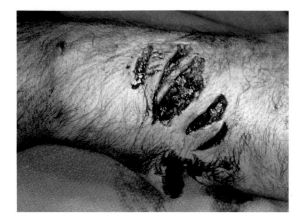

# SHARK VICTIMS

Bethany Hamilton was born to surf. She personifies the all-American dream. Like the other people who feature in this chapter, however, she belongs to an exclusive but unenviable club. Bethany was the victim of a devastating shark attack in which she lost an arm, and very nearly her life.

She was 13 years old. One morning in October 2003 Bethany was doing what she loves best − surfing off the coast of Hawaii's world-famous North Shore. What happened that day would change her life. Bethany was waiting for a wave; her left hand was dangling in the water. She never saw the shark. It was all a blur, she recalls. 'It was over in a few seconds. I remember the water around me turning bright red with my blood. Then I saw that my arm had been bitten off almost to the shoulder.'

Bethany is a girl who loves life and so she managed to push to the back of her mind the briefest of thoughts that she might actually die. Fortunately for the blonde teenaged surfer there were people on the beach whose prompt actions saved her life. A friend used a surf leash as a

tourniquet to stop the profuse bleeding from what was now just a stump.

The culprit on this occasion turned out to be a large tiger shark. The local people hunted down and killed the shark they claimed was responsible, saying the jaws were a perfect match.

Bethany's story instantly catapulted her into the headlines. Her remarkable recovery and desire to get back into the water made her a celebrity. Everybody wanted to know everything about her. She appeared on television shows around America and was interviewed endlessly by journalists from all over the world. There is no hint of blame in Bethany's attitude to her attacker. Her simple but mature philosophy is: 'Well, if your number is up...'

She argues that it is no use whatsoever constantly asking 'what if'? While some people injured in this way might have lost confidence or hidden away from public gaze, with the help of her family and friends Bethany rebuilt her life around the sport she adores. She even wrote a book about her experiences *Soul Surfer*. Bethany has overcome her terrible accident − she refuses to

wear her prosthetic arm – and competes with gusto in surfing events. But she knew from that day on she would forever be known as 'that surfer girl who got her arm bitten off by a shark.'

Why she was attacked is another matter. Sharks are not premeditated killers. It helps if we think about their normal prey and how they target it, then consider what a surfer must look like to a shark swimming below. The chances are that the surfboard with arms or legs dangling over the sides may look like a seal or a turtle. Since surfers account for a high proportion of shark victims, scientists are convinced that the majority of attacks are simply cases of mistaken identity. In many incidents the victim is left alone after the first 'bump and bite' because they are alien to the shark's usual diet.

Chris Sullivan, a teacher from Newquay in Cornwall, UK, was just such a casualty. He too had been surfing with friends while holidaying off Noordhoek in South Africa. It was another excellent day and the water was crystal clear. Suddenly Chris noticed a large, ominous shape beneath him. It was a great white shark and Chris knew he had to get out of the way. But the shark pulled him by the leg, dragging him along on his surfboard. Jokingly, Chris remarked 'I landed a few girly punches on it. I felt my leg slide out but the teeth were so sharp there was no pain.'

Chris was badly injured but he was lucky that he had no broken bones and his bleeding was not life-threatening. In fact, after catching a wave ashore, he managed to run up the beach – his wetsuit holding his torn leg together. Like Bethany, he was fortunate that there were people nearby who reacted with amazing speed to his injuries. Though he could see the damage, he was laughing and joking throughout his ordeal. Chris needed some 200 stitches in hospital and made an

**Previous pages**

Page 68: This bite was inflicted by a 6.5 feet (2m) long shark.

Page 69: Brave Bethany Hamilton smiles again after recovering from the shark attack while surfing off Hawaii North Shore. She refuses to use a prosthetic limb and is determined to live life to the full.

almost full recovery. Likewise, his story sparked a huge media interest. But the common theme proved to be a passion for the ocean which inspired him to get back in the water near his home in Cornwall, which is a magnet for surfers in the UK. Sure, says Chris, he cannot help but react to strange shadows in the water but then he quickly applies the 'rationale that says there are no sharks' – well, at least only harmless basking sharks!

Sharks had always fascinated Chris. Now he says he is more fascinated than ever and actively does what he can to get the message across that sharks are 'amazing, mysterious animals that need to be better understood.' Chris's quest to gain that better understanding led him to contact another victim of a great white attack in South Africa, someone with whom he came to share a rare but ultimately close bond of friendship.

Craig Bovim had tasked himself with catching lobster for Christmas lunch on December 24, 2002. Conditions in Scarborough were awful. There was a big swell and the visibility in the water was poor. But Craig was determined. While out snorkelling, a large great white shark started swimming alongside him so close that he could make out the incredible detail of every scar and blemish on its body. Sharks often bear scars either from mating or, as Craig believes in this case, from doing battle with another male.

Then he lost sight of it. 'I got really scared. Then I saw the fin coming straight toward me like a speed boat.' The shark bit down hard on Craig's forearms and started pulling him out to sea. Somehow Craig managed to battle free from the shark's razor-sharp teeth and in the process tore off a large chunk of muscle from his arm. He was also bitten badly on the leg. By the time Craig reached the shore, he was bleeding heavily and in desperate need of medical help. Many operations later, Craig has regained full use of his left arm but only 30 percent of his right arm.

Until the attack which so nearly claimed his life Craig says he had never thought much about sharks, even to the point of being embarrassed by his ignorance.

Because a large part of his life has been spent in the water, he realizes that statistically the chances of him encountering sharks are necessarily greater. The attack has had a profound impact on his life and he has set about trying to challenge the way sharks are treated by people. He is vehemently opposed to the craze for cage diving when using a chum bait. 'There used to be trophy hunters who killed sharks. Now we have people making money with shark tourism. Let's take the next step and do this with passive shark watching – without baiting the animals.'

Craig Bovim and Chris Sullivan take the view that no one can ever know for certain whether unnaturally feeding great whites can modify their behavior and so, in turn, increase the risk to humans. 'That being so, we shouldn't take the risk,' Craig argues. Even so, the risks are incredibly small. Statistically, we are more likely to be knocked down by a car, or be struck by lightning, than be bitten by a shark.

Tony White, an award-winning English underwater photographer, had set out to take pictures of an amazing phenomenon called the 'sardine run' in South Africa. This is when billions of these small fish migrate north along the coast and subsequently create a feeding frenzy among tens of thousands of predators – from dolphins and seabirds to tuna and sharks.

Tony nearly lost an arm within a few minutes of his first dive. His mistake, he says, was to position himself above a bait-ball of fish (a bait-ball is formed when thousands of fish swim tightly together for protection). When a bronze whaler shark came charging through the bait-ball to feast on this free bonanza, it caught Tony's arm with such force he was lifted out of the water. Tony's arm was saved thanks to a speedy transfer to hospital where the doctors were familiar with shark injuries. Tony, too, had to overcome his fears of getting back in the water to carry on his profession. But get in the water he did and with a message about which he remains passionate. 'The shark didn't attack me – it just bit me by mistake – as simple as that.'

For all the hype and sensationalism associated with shark victims over the years, the people who have actually been on the receiving end of those notorious teeth are often the first to defend them.

Perhaps the most famous shark victim in the world is the Australian Rodney Fox. In 1963, a great white shark caused him such terrible injuries it was a miracle he survived. He needed 462 stitches. His proud boast is that 'since then I have dedicated most of my life to the appreciation, preservation and research of the great white shark.'

Inevitably there will be other shark victims in the future. Doubtless man's primeval fear of and fascination with sharks will remain undimmed. But perhaps our understanding of the king of the blue wilderness will continue to improve and help us to preserve the domain of the shark.

Underwater photographer Tony White was taking pictures of a feeding frenzy in a bait-ball of sardines when a bronze whaler shark (*Carcharhinus brachyurus*) grabbed hold of his right arm and pushed him clear out of the sea. Tony's arm was stapled together around the elbow. He has made an excellent recovery but insists that it was not an attack. The shark simply 'bit me by mistake.'

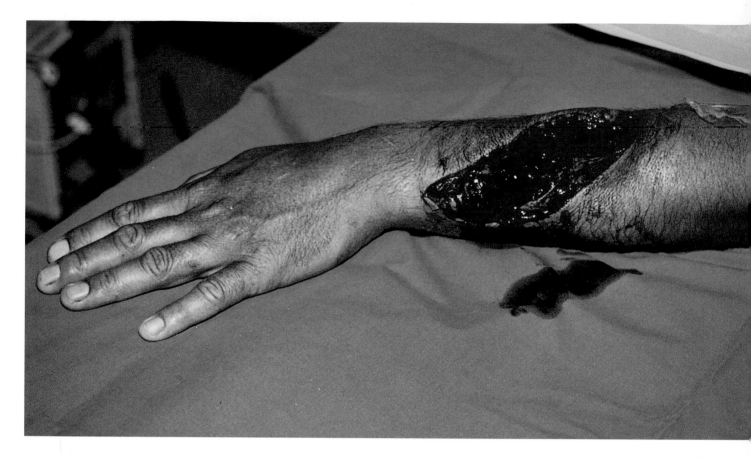

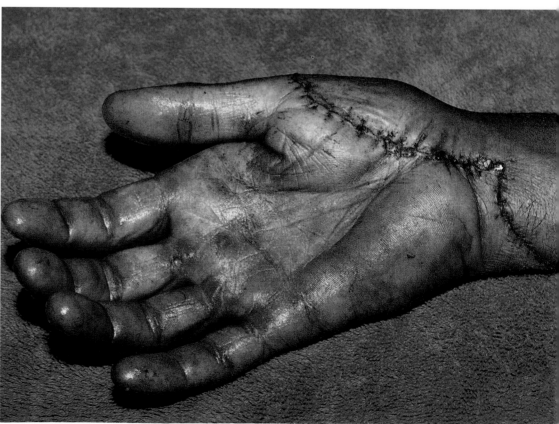

Craig Bovim nearly had his arms torn off by a great white while snorkelling near his home in South Africa. He still does not have full use of his right arm. He now uses his time to campaign for a more environmentally friendly approach to shark tourism.

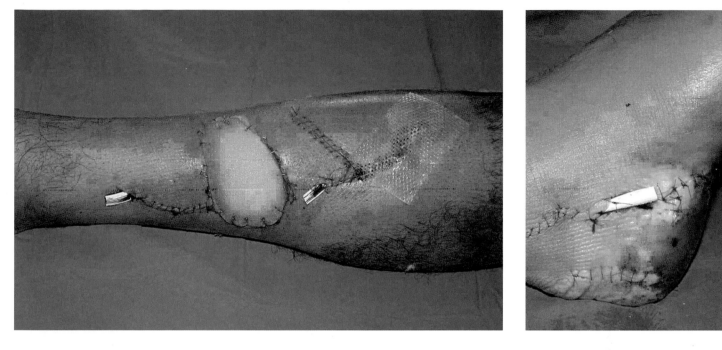

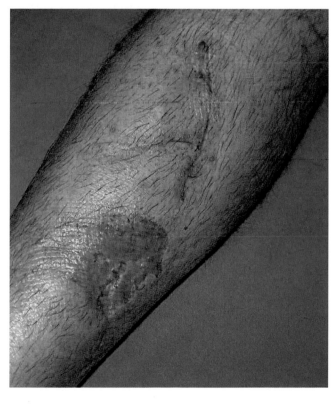

Chris Sullivan, a teacher from Newquay in Cornwall, UK, needed 200 stitches after a great white bit into his leg while surfing in South Africa. His fascination with sharks grew after the incident. 'They are amazing, mysterious animals that need to be better understood,' he says. Right: Chris and his partner, Barbara Robinson, pose with his shark-damaged surfboard and wetsuit.

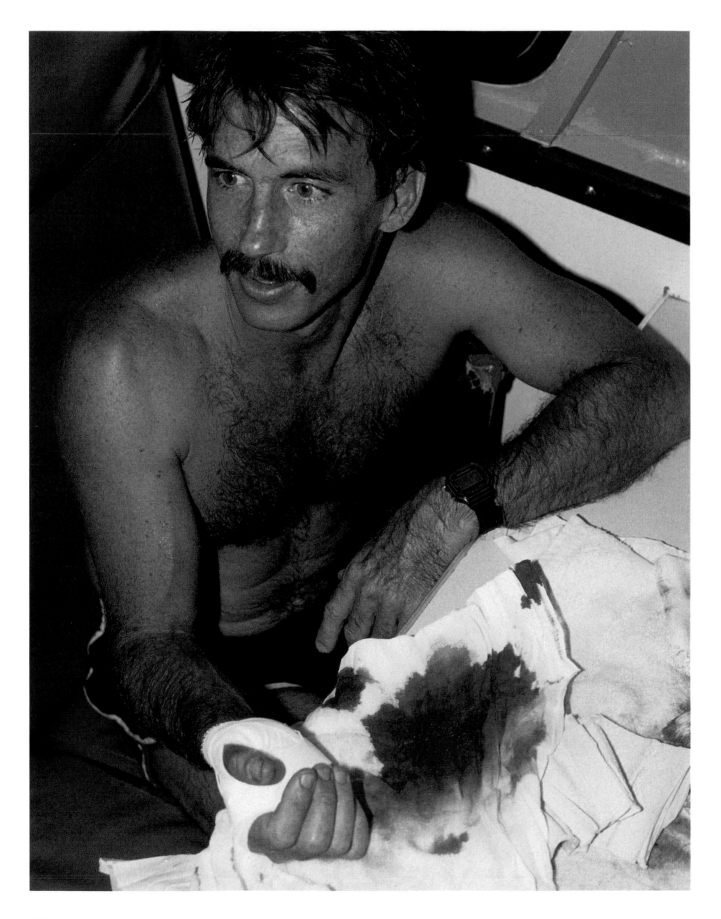

**Opposite:** Underwater photographer Doug Perrine receives treatment for a badly bitten hand after an attack by a Caribbean reef shark in the Bahamas in 1988.

**Right:** Seen from below, a surfer creates a silhouette similar to that of a seal or a turtle, possibly leading sharks to attack by mistake.

**Below:** Australian Rodney Fox became world famous as the victim of a great white shark attack in 1963 which nearly killed him. He needed more than 460 stitches to his arms and abdomen. Since then he has campaigned tirelessly on behalf of sharks, educating people about their place in the ocean hierarchy and trying to stop them being killed for shark fin soup.

# THE GREAT WHITE

When Steven Spielberg made the block-buster movie *Jaws*, he created a monster. That famously haunting 'dah-dum dah-dum' beat came to represent everything that is terrifying about the world's most notorious – and arguably most dangerous – carnivore in the ocean, the great white shark.

It is hard to believe when you see those large, razor sharp teeth protruding from its massive, extending jaw, that it is actually a big fish with a relatively small brain.

Great white sharks are also known by the names white pointer and white death. They are indeed super sharks in a league of their own. They have evolved over more than 100 million years with such finely honed killing instincts that it is no surprise that they are unrivaled in their status at the top of the marine food chain.

A large animal can grow to 21 feet (6m plus) in length and weigh in at a colossal 5000 pounds (2270kg). Scientists calculate that a great white shark is capable of exerting a lethal force of more than 20 tons per square inch when biting something. Folklore and legend would have us believe that there have been giant great white sharks more than 30 feet (9m) in length. One mythical creature off the coast of South Africa was supposedly so large it became known as the 'submarine with teeth.'

Almost always when we see pictures of great white sharks, the image is of a gaping mouth, bloodied snout, jet black eyes and, most frightening of all, jagged teeth so sharp they can slice the toughest of flesh like a knife through butter. They are undoubtedly fearsome killers capable of inflicting horrifying wounds. The film *Jaws* compounded the animal's reputation as a man-eater. The storyline was compelling. It was based on the notion that certain sharks deliberately stalk and hunt down human victims in an almost gratuitous fashion. The grisly sight of a lone swimmer being torn apart, as has happened in real life, sent shockwaves around the world. So profound was the impact of the movie, based on the best-selling Peter Benchley novel *Jaws*, that many thousands of sharks were killed by people – fueled by an irrational fear which reached fever pitch.

Looking every bit the ultimate killer of the oceans, a great white displays its pale underside as it swims close to the surface.

But the truth about 'Jaws' is only now beginning to emerge. Attacks by great white sharks are thankfully infrequent. In fact, sharks on average only kill about 12 people every year. The terrible nature of shark attacks and our grim fascination with horror means these deaths are often reported around the world in gory detail, with banner headlines.

Studies of shark behavior in places like southern Australia, South Africa, and the west coast of the United States – especially California – have revealed a wide range of behavior patterns. These provide vital clues about how and why the sharks attack in they way do.

Great whites have been shown to be incredibly stealthy creatures. Their staple diet

**Previous pages**

Page 76: The great white shark (*Carcharodon carcharias*) in all its glory as the number one predator.

Page 77: The dorsal fin of the great white shark is enough to cause panic among bathers when its surfaces near a beach.

tends to be fur seals and sea lions as well as fish such as tuna from which they derive a high fat content. But seals are highly agile and more than a match for their monstrous aggressor in the event of a chase. So the shark plays a tactical waiting game, hunting hidden from sight in the murky depths below. The shark looks for the tell-tale signs of a victim, perhaps one that is off its guard heading back to shore after feeding.

When the timing is right the shark hurtles to hit the seal on the surface with such a massive burst of speed it can cause the entire animal to breach. In a successful strike the seal is as good as dead following the initial attack. The shark then simply circles its quarry until it is safe to gorge on its prey. The last thing a great white shark needs is for an injured seal to damage its eyes. Some sharks have what is called a nictitating membrane which covers and protects the eye in the final throes of attack; however, the great white lacks this adaption and simply rolls back its eyes as a defense. But the shark may have to make any number of potentially damaging strikes before finally winning the day.

Great whites belong to a group called the mackerel sharks, which include the torpedo-like mako. They are warm-blooded, meaning they can generate additional body heat within their muscles. Since great whites are generally found in colder waters, a 10-degree Celsius increase in body temperature, boosting its speed and ability to react quickly, can make the difference between success and failure when in pursuit of a warm-blooded mammal.

Often television programs show great white sharks apparently attacking boats or biting shark cages. For a long time this behavior was regarded as proof that they will attack indiscriminately. But research has shown that in the final stages of a kill the shark relies almost enntirely on its hypersensitive snout. This is smothered in tiny cavities which can detect faint electrical impulses. At the very last minute, therefore, the shark can become overwhelmed and confused by the comparatively strong electromagnetic fields of the boat or metal cage. The instinct is to bite hard and, since sharks have no tongue, this is also how they 'taste.'

Humans are not actually 'very tasty' to sharks since they have a very low fat content compared with the shark's normal diet. It is also a misconception that great whites are the top man-eaters. In fact, they only account for between ten and 20 percent of shark attacks on people. Shark attacks are now widely regarded as cases of mistaken identity. So, despite the newspaper headlines, sharks are really not 'cold blooded killers' after all. *Jaws* the movie perpetuated this myth and, to this day, the blood-curdling cries of swimmers being eaten alive by great white sharks still ring in our ears.

When the author Peter Benchley wrote *Jaws* little was known about sharks. He freely admits that his work helped to demonize sharks and says that he could not write the same story now, knowing what we do about them. A diver for many years, Benchley has enjoyed the thrill of coming face to face with the great white – albeit from the safety of a cage in the blue waters of the Pacific.

He describes the encounters as humbling experiences with a fascinating animal. He cannot turn back the clock but, more than three decades after the film was released, he hopes that his enduring legacy will be to help in the fight to save the much-maligned and misunderstood great white shark from persecution and vilification.

Peter Benchley, the author of *Jaws*, just feet away from the animal he helped to demonize. With hindsight, he says he would not write the same book and is now an ardent fan of these supreme predators of the oceans.

**Above:** The spectacle of a 3000lb (1360kg) great white shark breaching has only been witnessed in recent years. Experts believe the shark charges at its intended prey from deep water with such speed that it ends up making a dramatic leap into the air. Great whites can be encouraged to breach by towing a simple wooden cut-out of a seal behind a boat.

**Right:** The famous jaws of a great white baring its large serrated teeth. The upper rows are used for slicing while the bottom teeth can lock onto its prey. Sharks have many rows of teeth. Each time they lose teeth in an attack, teeth in the rows behind simply move forward to replace them as if on a conveyor belt. It is estimated that a shark may use up to 5000 teeth in a lifetime.

Great whites often bear the scars of previous struggles for survival. Females may display wounds that have been caused by the males biting down on them during the fairly brutal process of mating, but males sometimes carry the scars of battling for supremacy within their communities.

Drama in the midst of a school
of jackfish as they flee the
jaws of a determined predator.

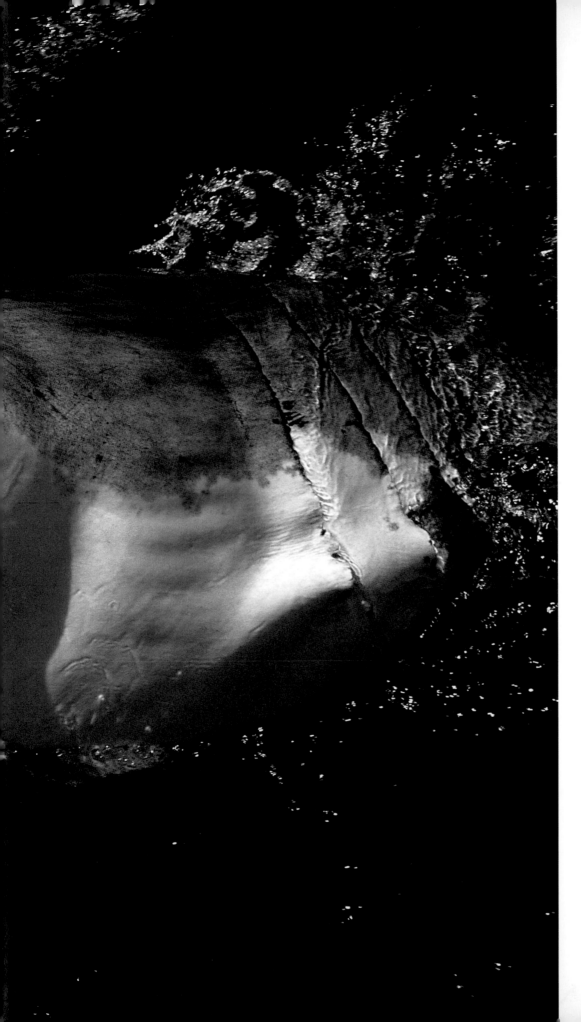

It is not uncommon for a great white to raise its head above the surface of the water. This is called spyhopping and demonstrates another of the shark's feats of agility when looking for food since surface-swimming mammals are part of its staple diet.

When great whites move in for the kill, they first use vision to locate their prey. As they get closer, they can roll back their jet black eyes to prevent injury from the sharp teeth or claws of marine mammals. It is then that the highly sensitive electro-receptors in the snout take over to enable them to precisely launch the final assault on their victims.

**Above:** The blue-gray coloring of this shark, allied to its white underbelly, provides excellent camouflage in the sea. People who have been attacked by great whites often only see them at the last minute. They are creatures of great stealth.

**Right:** There can be few more awesome sights than the mythical great white appearing in the flesh just a few feet from view. A cage is the best protection against jaws that can exert a force of 20 tons per square inch.

Studies of great white sharks made possible by baiting have helped dispel some of the myths about them. They are, in fact, thought to be social animals that live in groups with an established pecking order, which is especially evident when it comes to feeding. Females tend to be larger than males and are therefore the dominant sharks.

Douglas David Seifert's stunning pictures of a large great white off Guadalupe, Mexico, demonstrate why most of us have an innate fear of these huge ocean carnivores. But in a world which has been changed so radically by man, the great white is the most awesome reminder of a marine wilderness in which only the fittest and strongest survive.

# INDEX